GIRAFFES

A TRUE BOOK

by
Emilie U. Lepthien

Children's Press®
A Division of Grolier Publishing
New York London Hong Kong Sydney
Danbury, Connecticut

Reading Consultant
Linda Cornwell
Learning Resource Consultant
Indiana Department of
Education

A pair of giraffes

Library of Congress Cataloging-in-Publication Data

Lepthien, Emilie U.,
    Giraffes / by Emilie U. Lepthien.
        p.   cm.   —   (A true book)
    Includes bibliographical references and index.
    Summary: Describes the physical characteristics and habits of these
long-necked African animals.
    ISBN 0-516-20158-1 (lib. bdg.)   ISBN 0-516-26098-7 (pbk.)
    1. Giraffe—Juvenile literature.   [1. Giraffe.]   I. Title.   II. Series.
QL737.U56L46   1996]
599.73'57—dc20   96-13985
                                                                   CIP
                                                                    AC

Contents

The World's Tallest Animal

The giraffe is a mammal that lives in Africa. It is the world's tallest animal. Adult male giraffes can measure up to 11 feet (3.3 meters) tall—and that's just at the shoulder! With their very long necks, giraffes can measure nearly

20 feet (6 m) tall from their hooves to the top of their heads. Female giraffes are usually about 2 feet (0.6 m) shorter than the males.

The giraffe's unusual height makes it possible for it to eat food that most animals can't reach. It stretches its full length to eat the leaves, buds, and fruit on the tops of acacia trees and thorn trees.

Millions of years ago, giraffes must have roamed

Giraffes eating

Europe and Asia. Fossilized giraffe bones have been found in many places.

Giraffes live in Africa on grassy plains called savannas.

Today, though, giraffes live in Africa. They live in most African countries south of the Sahara desert. They like the savannas and grasslands, where they find their favorite trees and grasses.

What a Way To Eat

Giraffes have very interesting tongues. Their tongues can be as long as 18 inches (45 centimeters) long. Giraffe tongues are *prehensile*. Monkeys have prehensile tails. They can wrap their tails around branches and hang by them. Giraffes can wrap their

Giraffes use their long, flexible tongues to grasp leaves from the tops of trees.

tongues around high branches and strip off the leaves. Giraffes also eat grass, grains, and other plants. Their style of feeding is called *browsing*.

Mammals that feed on plant materials, have four stomachs, and chew their cud are called *ruminants*. Giraffes, cattle, sheep, goats, deer, and antelope are ruminants.

Like other ruminants, giraffes quickly swallow their food without chewing it very much. The food is held for a while in the animal's first stomach, where it is only partially digested. Later, when the giraffe is resting, it brings up small

lumps of food and chews them. This regurgitated food is called *cud*. After the cud is swallowed again, it goes through the second, third, and fourth stomachs, where it is completely digested.

Giraffes browse mostly in the early morning or late afternoon. They rest in the shade during midday. They may browse or chew their cud even after dark.

A giraffe resting at midday

From Head to Tail

Giraffes may be strange-looking animals, but some of their unique features help them survive in the wild. Their upper lips are long and muscular, so they can pull and tear tough leaves. The stiff hairs on their lips protect their mouths from the sharp thorns on acacia trees.

Giraffes have long lips covered with stiff, protective hairs.

Giraffes have eyes so wide-set that they can even see behind their heads. This helps giraffes spot enemies before they get too close.

Giraffes have large eyes
that stick out a little from
their heads. The placement of
their eyes allows them to see

all around—even behind their heads! This gives them a better chance of spotting a lion creeping up behind them.

Giraffes' necks are long, but they are actually somewhat stiff. Even though their necks are so long, they have only the usual seven neck vertebrae found in mammals. Even humans have seven neck vertebrae—and our necks are a lot shorter than a giraffe's!

When male giraffes fight, they swing their long necks and heads

Giraffes showing affection (left)
Giraffes fighting (below)

against each other. They usually fight for possession of females.

Sometimes male and female giraffes show they like each other by twining their necks around each other.

The giraffe's back slopes toward its long tail. The tail ends in a tuft of long black hairs. The animals use their tails to switch away insects from their backs.

A giraffe's tail

Long Legs

When you look at a giraffe, you might think that its front legs are longer than its hind legs. Actually, they are the same length. The giraffe's sloping back makes the front and back legs look different.

With such long legs, what a time they have taking a drink! They must spread their

Although it looks like a giraffe's front legs are longer than its back legs, they are actually the same length (left). To get a drink of water, a giraffe must spread its forelegs far apart (right).

forelegs far apart. Then they can bend their heads down to take a drink of water.

21

Like camels, giraffes are known for being able to go for a long time—as long as a month—without drinking. This is partly because they get moisture from the leaves they eat. Perhaps they know, too, that when they are drinking, they can easily be attacked by other animals. But if there is plenty of water and the giraffes feel safe, they drink every day.

Those long legs come in handy when a giraffe must escape an attacker. Giraffes

Though they may look a little awkward, giraffes are fast runners.

can run at speeds of 20 to 30 miles (32 to 48 kilometers) per hour. They can sometimes out-run a lion.

Although their best defense is to run, giraffes can also fight. They use their forelegs to strike an enemy with great force.

GREAT GALLOPING GIRAFFES!

Giraffes have an unusual gallop. When they run, they move both feet on one side of the body and then both feet on the other side. Horses, on the other hand, move the legs on the opposite sides of their body at the same time as they gallop. But even though the giraffe's gallop may look strange, it can run at speeds of up to 32 miles (48 km) per hour. That's pretty fast!

Coloring

Most giraffes' coats have dark spots on a light background. No two animals have the same markings. Some giraffes may be unspotted or almost all white or dark. The markings are protective coloration. They help to "hide" the

Three Rothschild's giraffes

animal from predators
when it is out on the savanna
or resting.

Coats of Many Colors

At first glance, it might seem that all giraffes look alike, but there are actually several different kinds of giraffes in Africa. Three of the most common are the Masai giraffe, the Rothschild's giraffe, and the Reticulated giraffe. Can you see the differences in their coats?

Masai giraffe

Rothschild's giraffe

Reticulated giraffe

Close-ups of giraffe skin

Giraffe hide is very tough. At one time, people killed the animals to make tough leather. They used the tuft of hairs on the tail for the ends of their arrows. Today, the giraffe is protected from hunting by law.

Cow and Calf

Female giraffes are called cows. Their babies are called calves. Male giraffes are called bulls.

Females usually have only one baby at a time. A calf is born about 14 or 15 months after a cow has mated with a bull. For 6 to 12 months after

A giraffe cow nursing her calf (left)
A cow and calf browsing for food (right)

its birth, the calf will feed on its mother's milk. It will stay close to its mother for more than a year.

Baby giraffes are quite a sight. They may weigh 130 pounds (58.5 kilograms) when they are born and stand almost 6 feet (1.8 m) tall! Giraffes reach their full height when they are about ten years old.

A young giraffe

Giraffe Troops

Giraffes like to live with other giraffes. Usually they live in small groups called troops. A troop generally has 6 to 12 animals. Cows and their calves are led by a mature bull in the troop.

The giraffes may also gather in small herds of 15 to 20 animals. It is rare to find herds of more than 50 animals.

Giraffes live in small groups called troops.

Sometimes, giraffes gather into herds of 15 to 20 animals.

At midday, the troop or
herd may be seen resting in
the open grasslands of the
savanna if there are no trees
close by. At night, they may
lie down or sleep standing up.

Giraffe Talk

For many years, people thought that giraffes made no sounds. They thought the animals had no voices.

Now we know that when they are frightened or angry, they make little whistling cries or grunts.

Scientists also think giraffes communicate with each other

35

in another way. They may use ultrasonic sounds to talk to each other. The sounds are too high pitched for humans to hear. The sound may be like those of high-pitched whistles that people use to call dogs.

Giraffa Camelopardalis

For many centuries, people have enjoyed watching giraffes in zoos and game parks around the world. Julius Caesar (left) brought giraffes to Rome to celebrate his victories in Africa 1,900 years ago. To create even greater interest in these strange creatures, he called them *camelopards*. He suggested they were a cross between a camel and a leopard. This, of course, is not true. But even today, the scientific name for the Common Giraffe is Giraffa Camelopardalis.

A Relative of the Giraffe

In 1901, scientists discovered that the giraffe had a relative, the okapi. The okapi is one of the world's rarest animals. Only a few have ever been captured and taken to zoos.

At first sight, you might not think that the okapi is related

The okapi, which also lives in Africa, is related to the giraffe.

to the giraffe. They look very different. When scientists first saw the animal in the forests of Uganda, they thought it looked like a horse. Then they thought it might be related to the zebra, because of its stripes.

An okapi's head (right) resembles that of its ancestor—an extinct short-necked giraffe (left) that lived millions of years ago.

It wasn't until 1901, when Sir Harry Johnston examined the skull of an okapi, that he found that it is a cousin of the giraffe. The skull resembled the fossils of the extinct short-necked giraffe that lived in Europe and Asia ten million years ago.

The okapi is also much shorter than the giraffe. It stands about 4 to 6 feet (1.2 to 1.8 m) tall. Like the giraffe, the okapi's body slopes toward the tail. The legs and part of the haunches are striped, providing protective coloration. Only the male okapi has horns.

Like the giraffe, the okapi uses its long, prehensile tongue to strip leaves, buds,

Like giraffes, okapis have long, prehensile tongues.

and fruit from trees. It also feeds on grasses and ferns. The okapi's tongue is so long that the animal can use it to clean its own eyes and eyelids! Okapis are nocturnal. This means that they are active mainly at night. During the day, okapis hide in the thick, dense rainforests of Zaire and Uganda.

The giraffe and the okapi are among the world's most interesting and unusual animals.

To Find Out More

Here are some additional resources to help you learn more about giraffes.

Books

Guggisberg, C.A.W., **The World of Animals: Giraffes.** Golden Press, 1969.

Lindblad, Lisa, **The Serengeti Migration.** Hyperion Books for Children, 1994.

MacClintock, Dorcas, **A Natural History of Giraffes.** Charles Scribner's Sons, 1973.

Sattler, Helen Roney, **Giraffes, The Sentinels of the Savannas.** Lothrop, Lee & Shepard Books, 1989.

Switzer, Merebeth, **Our Wildlife World: Giraffes.** Grolier, 1988.

Organizations

Sierra Club
730 Polk Street
San Francisco, CA 94109
415-776-2211
http:/ww.sierraclub.org/

Smithsonian: National Zoological Park
3000 block of Connecticut Avenue, NW
Washington, DC 20008
202-673-4800
http:/www.si.sgi.com/ perspect.afafam/afazoo.htm

African Wildlife Foundation
1717 Massachusetts
  Avenue, NW
Washington, DC 20036
202-265-8393
*http://www.rhinochasers.
com/awf/index.html*

**Giraffe at the
Knoxville Zoo**
*http://loki.ur.utk.edu/ut2kids
/zoo/giraffe.html*

Giraffe Cam
*http://www.ceram.com/
cheyenne/giraffe.html*

Plains Biome
*http://estel.uindy.edu/out
Reach/guestSchools/
indyzoo/news/plains.html*

Reticulated Giraffe
*http://www.blum.tis.net/zoo
/animals/giraffe.html*

Giraffe Factsheet
*http://www.fwl.org/seaba/
members/oz/fact.giraffe.
html*

Important Words

digested changed into a form that can be absorbed by the body

extinct no longer in existence

forelegs the front legs of an animal

fossil the remains of a plant or animal of an earlier age, hardened and preserved in earth or rock

mammal any of a group of animals that have vertebrae, are warm-blooded, produce milk for their young, and have hair

prehensile able to seize or grasp by wrapping around

savanna a grassy plain with few or no trees

ultrasonic having to do with sounds that are above the range of human hearing

vertebrae the bones that form the backbone in animals such as fish, reptiles, amphibians, birds, and mammals

Index

Meet the Author

Emilie U. Lepthien received her B.A. and M.S. degrees and certificate in school administration from Northwestern University. She taught upper-grade science and social studies, and was a school principal in Chicago, Illinois, for twenty years. For Children's Press, she has written books in the *Enchantment of the World*, *True Book*, and *America the Beautiful* series.